#01

Art:
Yuuki Kodama

Original Story:
Otaro Maijo
•The Detectives United

#01 ENTRANCE

Contents

GABA (JOLT)

SOME COUNTRY ROAD—ONE I'M SURE I'VE NEVER SEEN BEFORE.

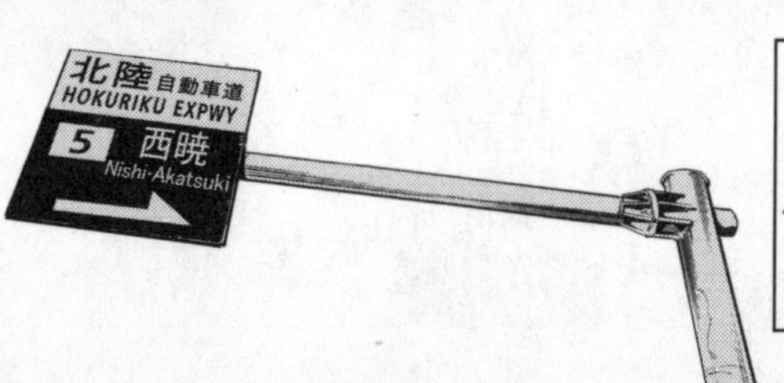

WHAT AM I DOING PARKED HERE...?

西暁
Nishi-Akatsuki
NISHI... AKATSUKI ...?

THE NAME DOESN'T RING ANY BELLS.
THIS IS NO USE. I DON'T KNOW ANYTHING ...

EH?
WAIT, SLOW DOWN. ANY-THING?
COME TO THINK OF IT, WHO AM I...?

I DON'T EVEN KNOW MY OWN NAME!
GAPA (CLUNK)
WHO THE HELL AM I...? IS THERE ANYTHING HERE THAT COULD HELP IDENTIFY ME...?

NOTHING IN THE DASH... HOW ABOUT A WALLET?
SA (SHWIP)
SA
SA
SA
SA
NOPE... THERE'S NOTHING ON ME.
HM? DOES THAT MEAN I WAS DRIVING WITHOUT A LICENSE?
PAAA (HOOONK)
GASHAAN (SMASH)
HUH?

WHAT WAS THAT? SOUNDED LIKE A HORN AND A...
ドオオオン
DOOON (BOOM)
AH!
パァ パ パ パ パァ
PAA PA PA PA PAA
AN ACCIDENT!?

ドッ
DO (JAM)

ガゴッ
GAKO (CLUNK)

グッ
GU (STOMP)

...UH, ME? WHY AM I GOING TO THE CRASH EXACTLY?

LEAVING ASIDE THAT I'M DRIVING WITHOUT A LICENSE, IS THERE ANYTHING I CAN DO THERE?

IS IT TO HELP THE INJURED? DOESN'T FEEL LIKE I HAVE MUCH MEDICAL KNOWLEDGE...

LOOKS LIKE I KNOW HOW TO DRIVE, AT LEAST.

I JUST FLOORED IT WITHOUT EVEN KNOWING WHY. GUESS I'LL SEE WHAT HAPPENS WHEN I GET THERE.

WHAT'S THE DEAL WITH THIS INTER-CHANGE ...?
IT'S UNMAN-NED?
IS IT SET UP SO YOU CAN GET ON AND OFF THE MAIN ROAD FREELY?

STILL, THIS CAR HAS AN ETC CARD. I SHOULD BE ABLE TO GET ON THE EXPRESSWAY QUICKLY.
OH, AND I KNOW WHAT AN ETC CARD IS—ELECTRONIC TOLL COLLECTION.

THAT'S IT...

福井 Fukui

BY ACTING, I MIGHT BE ABLE TO REMEMBER WHO I AM, PIECE BY PIECE!

PI (BIP)

IN WHICH CASE... MY LITTLE RESCUE MISSION NOW HAS MEANING!

!

ゴォオオオ
GOOOOO (VRRM)
オオオオ
OOOOO (WHOOOOSH)
GOTTA HELP THEM...
I'LL ARRANGE FOR AN AMBULANCE AND OTHER EMERGENCY SERVICES.
ゴォオオ
GOOOO
THEN I'LL GO ALONG TO THE HOSPITAL AND CONSULT SOMEONE ABOUT MY OWN ISSUE.

グオオオオ
GUOOOO
(BWAAAA)
バアアア
BAAAAA
(HONK)
バッバアアア
BABBAAAA
!?
ド
DO
(WHAM)

GIAAAA
(SCREECH)
...!
WHAT THE HELL WAS THAT...!?
PI
(BLIP)
BUON
(VROOM)

I'LL WRITE DOWN THEIR LICENSE PLATES AND CALL THE POLICE...! EXCEPT I DON'T HAVE A CELL PHONE.

THEN WHY AM I CHASING THEM?

I RUSHED OFF ON IMPULSE AGAIN!

BUT I CAN'T IGNORE TWO DUMP TRUCKS RUNNING PEOPLE OVER AT A HUNDRED AND TWENTY KLICKS RIGHT BEFORE MY EYES...

BAAAA (HONK)

BAAAA

GOOOO (VRM)

SEEMS LIKE I'VE GOT A STRONG SENSE OF JUSTICE.

?

WHAT'S THAT?

THERE'S A STATION WAGON AHEAD OF THE DUMP TRUCKS.
BAAAAA
BAAAA
BAAA
ARE THEY HONKING AT THAT STATION WAGON THIS TIME?
BABBAAA
OOOO (WHOOOSH)
BUT WHY ...?
ARE... ARE THEY TRYING TO TELL HIM TO MOVE?

WHAT THE HELL ARE THESE BASTARDS PLAYING AT!?
プァッ
PUA (HONK)
ププァ〜ッ
PUAAA
オオオ
OOO (WHOOSH)
プァァァーッ
PUAAAA
ギュウゥ
GYUUU (GRIND)
オオオオ
プァーッ
PUAAA
HEY!
DO YOU GUYS HAVE ANY IDEA WHAT YOU'RE DOING!?
SLOW DOWN!

...!

STOP...! HOLD THE SPEED YOU'RE AT!

WHAT THE HELL?

WHY'S HE TELLING ME WHAT TO DO?

WHAT ARE YOU TALKING ABOUT!? JUST SLOW DOWN!

LISTEN! DON'T GO ANY FASTER THAN THAT!

GOO (RRM)

WE'LL PULL OUT IN FRONT!

BUOOO (VROOO)
HEY! STOP!
PULL OVER TO THE SHOULDER!
カス カス
SFX: SUKA (FSSH) SUKA
?
OOOO (WHOOSH)
MY BRAKES AREN'T ...!?

THAT WAS CLOSE!

GYA (SCREECH)
GYA

HEY, YOU OVER THERE!
WHEW!

WHAT'S GOING ON WITH THE DUMP TRUCKS BEHIND US!?

I DON'T KNOW!
BUT WATCH OUT! SOUNDS LIKE THEY DON'T PLAN ON STOPPING!

ARE THEY OUT OF THEIR MINDS !?
WHILE THAT'S POSSIBLE...
...HE DIDN'T SEEM INSANE TO ME...

BUROOO (VROOO)

I DON'T KNOW! I DON'T EVEN KNOW WHO I AM!
WHAT !?

I SAID TOO MUCH.
I'M STARTING TO PANIC TOO.

HEY, YOU!
WHAT ARE YOU DOING!?
MY BRAKES AREN'T WORKING!

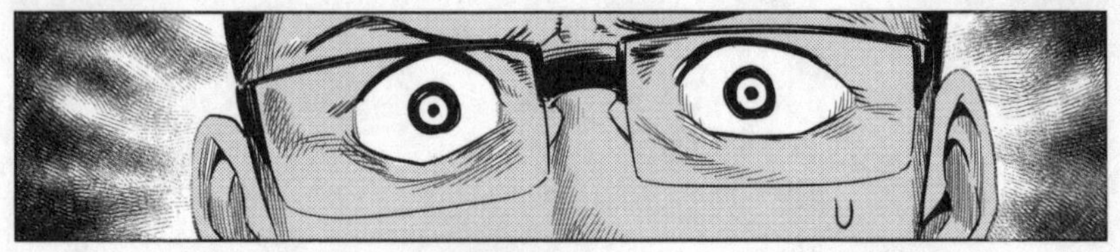

I—
P
i
南条
Nanjo
5-1
ETC
出口
EXIT
EV QUICK
コンビニ
24H
I'M GETTING OUT OF HERE! SO LONG!
!

BAAAA (HONK)
OOO (WHOOSH)
BAAA
BAAAA
...
DOOOOON (KABOOM)
...!?
WHAT'S HAPPENING?

...BECAUSE THEIR BRAKES ARE BROKEN TOO?

ZU (SHOOM)

AND IT WOULD EXPLAIN THAT DRIVER'S ATTITUDE.

THERE'S NO MALICIOUS INTENT TO HIS ACTIONS.

SUKA
SUKA (FSSH)
ARE WE ALL VICTIMS OF THE SAME SITUATION...
...STUCK IN A STATE OF PANIC?

BUT HOW IS IT POSSIBLE FOR THE BRAKES ON OUR VEHICLES ...
GOOOO (VRM)
...TO ALL FAIL AT THE SAME TIME?

THIS CAR IS THE TYPE THAT CAN BE CONTROLLED REMOTELY VIA A NETWORK CONNECTION.

EVEN IF MY CAR WAS HACKED AND IT WAS POSSIBLE FOR A HACKER TO GAIN ACCESS TO THE BRAKE CONTROLS...

STILL, THAT FEATURE IS FOR ACCIDENT PREVEN-TION.

YOU SHOULDN'T BE ABLE TO USE IT TO KILL ONLY THE BRAKES.

OOO (WHOOSH)

...THE DUMP TRUCKS BEHIND ME ARE TOO OLD TO BE EQUIPPED WITH ANYTHING LIKE THAT.

SHIT!
NOT ONLY HAVE I LOST MY MEMORIES, I...HAVE NO IDEA HOW OR WHY THIS IS HAPPENING.

129.7km/h
COULD THERE BE A CONNECTION BETWEEN MY AMNESIA AND THIS MASS BRAKE FAILURE?

I DON'T KNOW THAT EITHER.
GOOOO (VRM)
NO MATTER HOW MUCH I CHEW ON THIS IN MY HEAD, I PROBABLY WON'T FIND ANY ANSWERS.

WELL, FINE.
OOO (ROAR)
LET'S LOOK AT THE FACTS ALONE.

I'M CURRENTLY DRIVING A MALFUNC-TIONING VEHICLE.

FOR NOW, PRACTICALLY SPEAKING, I HAVE TO SURVIVE MY PRESENT SITUATION.
GYU (GRIP)
FIRST, THERE'S THREE WRECKS ...

OOOO (WHOOSH)
...I HAVE TO DODGE!!
BUON (VROOM)
ONE!!
NEXT IS ON THE RIGHT!
NO, DON'T PANIC! JUST STEER ...
...NICE AND EASY ...!!
I RAN OVER SOME-THING... I'M IN THE AIR!!
URGH!!
THAT'S TWO...!
BAKII (CRACK)

THERE'S NO WAY!!
WHICH WAY FOR THIS? RIGHT? LEFT?
OOO (WHOOSH)
HUH?
FINE.
GUO (LURCH)
IF THERE'S NOTHING TO LOSE ...
GYUA (SCREECH)
DOU (WHAM)
GAGAGA (KRRK)
AAAAA-AAAH!!

BUON (VROOM)

IT'S A MIRACLE!!

BUT... I CAN'T EXPECT MY LUCK TO HOLD OUT FOREVER.

EVEN MORE WRECKS KEEP PILING UP IN FRONT OF ME.
DOOOON (BOOM)
WHICH MEANS THERE'S GOING TO BE MORE AND MORE OBSTACLES.

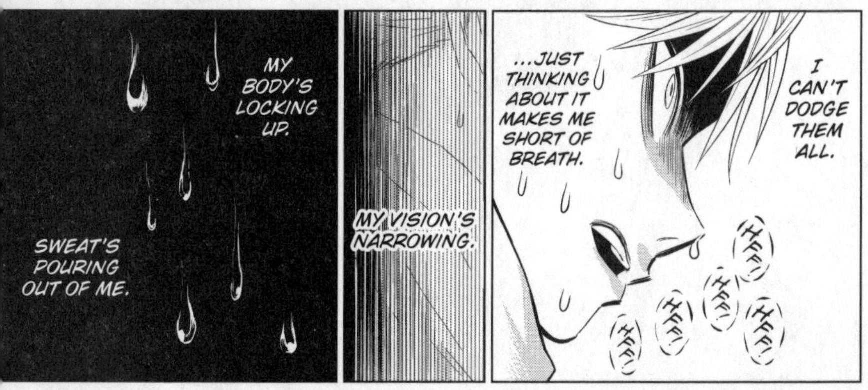

I CAN'T DODGE THEM ALL.
...JUST THINKING ABOUT IT MAKES ME SHORT OF BREATH.
MY VISION'S NARROWING.
MY BODY'S LOCKING UP.
SWEAT'S POURING OUT OF ME.

NOT GOOD...
DOOOON (BOOM)
AT THIS RATE, I'LL DIG MY OWN GRAVE.
KI (GLARE)
THINK.
DON'T WASTE BRAIN-POWER ON THE IRRELE-VANT.
OO (WHOOSH)
DON'T LET ADRENA-LINE TAKE OVER.
RECLAIM CONTROL OF YOUR BRAIN AND YOUR LIMBS.
GYU (GRIP)
GOOAA (VRM)

BUT AT THIS SPEED, IF I TURN TOO SHARPLY, THE CAR COULD EASILY ROLL OVER LIKE IT ALMOST JUST DID.

DO IT SLOWLY...

SLO—

BALIN (BWAM)

GYA
GYA
GYA
GYA (SCREECH)
RAAAAAAAAAAH!!!
GUH ...!
DODGED IT BY THE SKIN OF MY TEETH!
128.3
I'VE STARTED TO LOSE SOME SPEED!
AND— THERE WE GO!
HOLD TOGETHER FOR ME, MYSTERY CAR!
GYA
GYA
GYA
GYA
ONLY PROBLEM IS...

...IF I KEEP SLOWING DOWN, THE DUMP TRUCKS BEHIND ME WILL...

!

THAT'S THE CAR I DODGED!

GOOOO (RRRM)

GYA GYA GYA GYA GYA

NICE! WITH THAT WRECK DRAGGING IN FRONT OF THEM, THE DUMP TRUCKS ARE DECELERATING AS WELL.

THERE YOU GO. KEEP AT IT!

IF WE CAN BOTH KEEP LOSING SPEED, WE... CAN...

TA (TAP)
TATATTA
SELF-DRIVING MODE
ON
PI (BIP)
BAN (BAM)
DON (WHAM)
!?

YOU OKAY !?

......
...RIGHT, OF COURSE YOU AREN'T OKAY...
"ARE YOU OKAY"?
WHAT AM I EVEN SAYING...?
THINK YOU CAN GET OUT?

AM I OKAY? IN THE HEAD? WHAT AM I DOING ...?
THERE'S GETTING CAUGHT UP IN THE MOMENT, AND THEN THERE'S WHATEVER THIS IS!

I CAN'T!!
I'M TIRED OF BEING SCARED! I'M TIRED OF STRUGGLING! I CAN'T TAKE IT ANYMORE!
JUST LEAVE ME TO DIE!!
I DON'T KNOW THE FIRST THING ABOUT MYSELF.

HA HA...
BUT...
WELL, I'M HERE ALREADY... I'LL WAIT.
DO ME ONE FAVOR.
STRETCH OUT YOUR ARM...
...AND GRAB MY HAND.
IF YOU WERE BEING GENEROUS, YOU COULD CALL THIS... SOMETHING ALONG THE LINES OF BRAVERY.

MAYBE I'M A GUY WHO HAS SOME OF THAT...
YOU CAN HANDLE THAT, RIGHT?
IT'S NOT TOO HARD...
...OKAY.

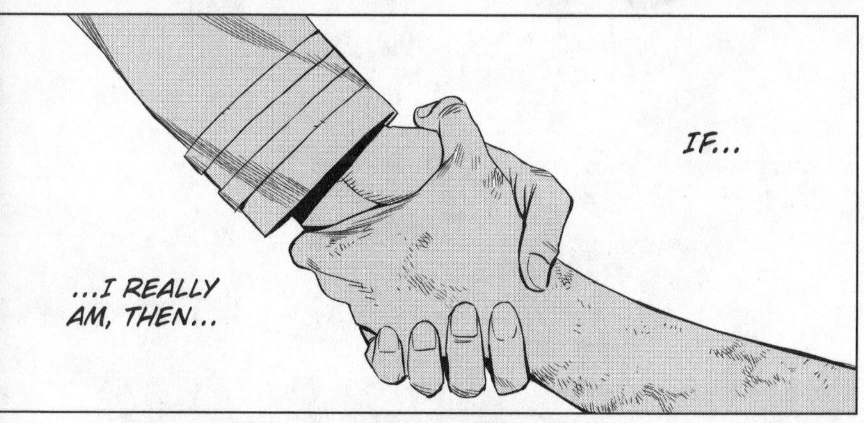
IF...
...I REALLY AM, THEN...

...WHAT I'M DOING ISN'T SOME BIG MISTAKE.
ドゴオォ
DOGOOO (CRASH)
HOLD ON TIGHT!

GU (LIFT)
GRAAAAH!
BAUN (FWISH)
DA (TMP)
DA
DA
ZUZAAAAA (SLIDE)
OO (WHOOSH)

DOOOOO (CRUNCH)
GYA
GYA (SCREECH)
ZA (THUMP)
DO (BAM)
......

OOO (WHOOSH)

DAMMIT! THE DRIVER'S SEATS ARE CRUMPLED LIKE PAPER...

......

IT'S PROBABLY TOO LATE FOR BOTH OF THOSE DRIVERS...

...UM... YOUR BACK...

ARE YOU OKAY?

HUH?

THERE'S SO MUCH BLOOD...

BUT I'M NOT INJURED...

...AM I?

HUH?

BETTORI (SOAKED)

OOO

WHAT IS THIS ...?

DAMN, BUDDY! THOSE WERE SOME MOVES!

P-POPS... SORRY. THE OTHER TRUCK DRIVER IS...
OO
YOU MEAN BILLY? WEREN'T NOTHING EITHER OF US COULDA DONE ABOUT THAT!
ALSO, I'M ONLY FORTY!
WHO YOU CALLIN' "POPS"!!?
GOOOO (VRM)
ANYWAY, GOOD ON YOU FOR SAVING THE WOMAN...
...BUT DID YOU DO SOMETHIN' TO THAT OTHER GIRL!?
WHAT OTHER GIRL?
THE GIRL IN THE TRUNK OF YOUR CAR.
THE ONE COVERED IN BLOOD!
I DON'T KNOW ANYTHING ABOUT A GIRL...
I TOOK OFF IN THAT CAR ON PURE IMPULSE AFTER WITNESSING AN ACCIDENT...
...STILL NOT KNOWING WHO I WAS—OR EVEN IF THE CAR WAS MINE.
I NEVER EVEN NOTICED THERE WAS SOMEONE THERE...!

GOOOO (VRM)

OOOOO (WHOOSH)

ZUZU (SSK)

DON'T TELL ME YOU...

...INJURED THAT GIRL OR SOMETHING?
HECK, SHE DIDN'T EVEN LOOK ALIVE TO ME!!

SORRY...

...BUT I...WOKE UP TEN MINUTES AGO...
...WITH NO MEMORY... OF ANYTHING UNTIL RIGHT BEFORE I GOT ON THIS HIGHWAY...

NOT EVEN OF WHO I AM.
LOOK AT YOUR DRIVER'S LICENSE!
I DON'T EVEN HAVE A WALLET.
YOU WERE DRIVIN' WITHOUT A LICENSE!?
I KNOW, RIGHT?
THIS AIN'T THE TIME TO CRACK JOKES ...!

WELL... IF A COP COMES ACROSS THIS, I'LL HOLD MY WRISTS OUT AND LET THEM CUFF ME.
HELL, MAYBE THE POLICE COULD DIG UP MY RECORDS FOR ME SOMEHOW.
THEY MIGHT EVEN FIND THE FAMILY I'M SEARCHING FOR...

......
I HAVE A FEELING THAT ISN'T GOING TO HAPPEN, THOUGH...
...YOU DON'T LOOK LIKE A MURDERER TO ME.

BESIDES, IF YOU REALLY WERE A MURDERER...

...I DON'T THINK YOU'D HAVE SAVED MY LIFE...

......

SHE'S GOT A POINT...

SO WHAT, YOU'RE AN AMNESIAC?

...I DON'T KNOW.

AT ANY RATE...

A BODY OF A GIRL?

DID I PUT HER THERE?

...I HAVE TO GET BACK TO MY CAR.

HOW?

I GOTTA WARN YA— AT THIS SPEED, EVEN CHANGING LANES COULD FLIP US... IF WE GO ANY FASTER...

YOU DON'T HAVE TO DO ANYTHING FOR ME.

...BUT THANKS ANYWAY.

WHAT'S YOUR NAME, POPS?

I TOLD YOU, I'M ONLY FORTY!

AND IT'S KENNY!

I'M TINA.

OKAY. KENNY AND TINA.

GOOO (VRM)

I WANT YOU TWO TO FOCUS ON YOUR OWN SURVIVAL ONLY.

HUH? BUT...

ブロオオオ
BUROOOOO (VROOOM)

LET ME ON TOO!

THE DUMP TRUCK IS STURDY, AND IT'S MOVING AT A SLOWER SPEED THAN HIS OWN CAR... I CAN SEE WHY IT WOULD LOOK MORE APPEALING.

STAY AT THAT SPEED! PULL UP TO THE SIDE!

I'LL COME TO YOU!

ガッ
GA (GRIP)

HUH?

KEEP YOUR HANDS ON THE STEERING WHEEL!

ゴオオオ
GOOOO (VRRM)

OPEN THE PASSENGER'S SIDE WINDOW!

トッ
TO (THUMP)

スルッ
SURU (SLIDE)
WHAT THE HELL ARE YOU DOING!? HOW IS YOU RIDING ALONG GONNA HELP!?
I'M GOING TO TAKE THE WHEEL FOR YOU.

OOO
(WHOOSH)
THANKS, TINA!
DO YOUR BEST TO STAY ALIVE WITH HIM!
GOOD LUCK!
...!
GOOD LUCK TO YOU TOO!
RIGHT!
BUROOO
(VROOOM)

I DON'T KNOW WHO I AM.

THE BRAKES ON MY CAR AND MY IMPULSES DON'T WORK, BUT I'VE RACED THIS FAR ON THEM NONETHELESS.

BUT THEN THERE'S THE GIRL IN THAT TRUNK...

GOOOO (VRM)

THIS DRIVE TO MAKE MY WAY TO HER IS MORE THAN SOMETHING SPUR-OF-THE-MOMENT...

I'LL ONLY GET A SECOND TO LOOK INTO THE TRUNK...

AA (FWOO)

GYULULU (PRESS)

FASTER...

GOAAA (RATTLE)

130

140

150

I HAVE TO GET TO HER!

!?
ドオッ
DOO (BOOM)
ス…
SU (SHMM)

DO (WHAM)
GYURU (SPIN)
OO (WHOOSH)

オオォオォオ
OOOOOOO
(WHOOSH)

IN THAT INSTANT—
KAERU-CHAN...

I REMEMBER WHO I AM.

MY NAME IS... SAKAIDO.

I'M THE BRILLIANT DETECTIVE.

I HAVE TO SOLVE THE MYSTERY OF KAERU-CHAN'S DEATH.
バアアア
BAAAA (HONK)
バアアアア
BAAAA
GYA (SCREECH)
ギャギャギャギャ
GYA
GYA
オォォォ
OOO (WHOOSH)
バアアアア
BAAAAA
バババアアアァ
BABBAAAA

BAAAAAA
DO (CRUNCH)

GABA (JOLT)

HAAH!

HFF!

HFF!

...Momoki-san. What's the status of the case?

ZUZUU (SHUM)

STILL SEARCHING FOR THE KILLER'S LOCATION WHILE WE INVESTIGATE THEIR IDENTITY.

THIS RUN...
...WAS THE FIRST TIME I MANAGED TO LOCATE KAERU-CHAN...
On your seventh try. Took long enough.
We're making more deductions about the case as well...but we need more information.

I CAN KEEP GOING.
...KEEP DYING.
ALL RIGHT... NO BREAK, THEN. DIVE BACK INTO THE *ID WELL*.

北陸自動車道
HOKURIKU EXPWY
5 西暁
Sakaido is awake.
パチッ
PACHI (BLINK)
END

#02 FIRST DAY

TOKYO METROPOLITAN POLICE DEPARTMENT (MPD)
BURORORO (VROOM)
HELLO THERE! OVER HERE.
BII
DETECTION
検知
BII (BREEP)
BII
YIKES!

DEEN (DUN)

SORRY! ARE YOU OKAY!? FUKUSEN-KUN!?

AH...HA-HA... THAT'S ME. PLEASURE TO MEET YOU...

YOU'RE EXACTLY LIKE I HEARD...
...HONDOU-MACHI-SAN.
AH HA HA...
DID MATSUOKA-SAN TALK ABOUT ME?
WELL, YEAH. BASICALLY, "BRILLIANT BUT CAN GET TUNNEL VISION, SO STAY ON YOUR TOES."
OW, OW, OW...
ANYWAY, I'LL DRIVE.
WHAT? WHY?
I'LL DO IT!
ARE YOU REALLY ASKING THAT AFTER CAUSING AN ACCIDENT A FEW SECONDS AGO...?
NO ARGUING! GET IN THE PAS-SENGER'S SIDE.
AHEM!
......
DO AS YOUR SENPAI SAYS.

ブロロロ
BUROROR0 (VROOM)
SORRY ABOUT THAT. THE WAKUMUSUBI SUDDENLY PICKED UP A READING AND I GOT DISTRACTED.
カチャ
KACHA (CHAK)

OH MAN, SO THIS IS ONE OF THOSE... WAKUMUSUBI, WAS IT?
YUP.
THAT ONE'S BEEN ISSUED TO YOU, SO GO AHEAD AND FAMILIARIZE YOURSELF WITH IT.
WAIT, THIS IS MINE?

UH-HUH. I FORGOT TO POWER IT OFF AFTER THE OPERA-TIONAL CHECK...
HM...? SO IF THE WAKUMUSUBI ACTIVATED...
...DOES THAT MEAN IT DETECTED A DRIVE TO KILL?

ISN'T THERE A NEW MURDER CASE, THEN?
AH...NO, YOU'RE WAY OFF. DON'T SCAN WITH IT AT RANDOM IN THIS AREA.
HUH? WHY IS THAT?

THE WAY COGNITION PARTICLES WORK, THE STRONGER THE DRIVE TO KILL...
...THE LONGER THE PARTICLES' LIFETIME.

HISTORICAL SAMURAI AND SOLDIERS HAD INCREDIBLE DRIVES TO KILL.
SO THE WAKUMUSUBI WILL PICK UP ALL KINDS OF OLD, PROBLEMATIC PARTICLES IN THIS AREA.

AH-HA-HA! THAT'S WILD!
THEN IF YOU WENT TO KYOTO, COULD YOU CREATE AN ID WELL FROM SHINSENGUMI COGNITION PARTICLES?
IT'D BE COOL TO FIND OUT WHO REALLY KILLED RYOUMA SAKAMOTO!
......
I DON'T GIVE A DARN ABOUT HISTORICAL MYSTERIES OR THE ID WELLS OF FAMOUS FIGURES.

OUR JOB IS TO CATCH KILLERS COMMITTING MURDERS IN THE HERE AND NOW.

OOOH, WE'VE GOT A VIEW OF MY NEW WORKPLACE!
OOO (WHOOSH)
SO THAT'S THE "KURA"...? LOOKS TOTALLY INCONSPICUOUS FROM THE OUTSIDE!
VUUN (VUM)
HUH?
HEY, I DON'T REMEMBER TURNING THIS ON...
THAT'S FUNNY.
WHAT'S GOING ON WITH IT?
A FORCED START-UP...!
KIKII (SCREECH)

HUH? WHAZZAT? WHAT'S GOING ON?
OOO (WHOOSH)
GOOD MORNING. THIS IS HONDOU-MACHI.
WE'VE DETECTED UNRECORDED COGNITION PARTICLES.
THE LOCATION IS NIITSU OOHASHI BRIDGE.
......
GABA (RUSTLE)
A NEW ID WELL...
GARAAAN (EMPTY)
UN-RECORDED COGNITION PARTICLES MEANS... HUH?
A NEW MURDER CASE? HERE?
THIS BRIDGE IS EXPOSED TO THE SEA BREEZE.
THE PARTICLES MAY HAVE BEEN BLOWN HERE FROM ANOTHER LOCATION.

EVEN SO... IT MEANS THERE'S A CRIME SCENE NEAR HERE.
MOMOKI-SAN.
GOOOO (FWOOSH)
Com-mencing investi-gation.
KURA HEADQUARTERS, WELLSIDE

OOO (WHOOSH)
BE CAREFUL, HONDOU-MACHI.
WE'RE DISPATCHING ASSISTANCE FROM THE METRO POLICE AND THE FIELD ANALYSIS TEAM.
ID WELL CONSTRUC-TION IS COMPLETE.

AND NARIHI-SAGO?
BEING TRANSFERRED FROM HIS CELL AS WE SPEAK.
ZA (STEP)

OOOOOO
ZA
ZA

ZA

THAT'S WEIRD...

OOOOOO
(WHOOOOSH)
WE'VE JUST BEEN CIRCLING AROUND AN AREA WITH CONCENTRATED COGNITION PARTICLES.
JIJI
(CRACKLE)
JIJI
I CAN'T PINPOINT THE CRIME SCENE.

PAISEN.
HOW MUCH WIND DOES IT TAKE TO CARRY COGNITION PARTICLES?
"PAISEN" ......?

GOOOO
(VRM)
'COS IT'S PRETTY WINDY TODAY...
I'LL TRY TO RUN A SIMULATION USING THE CURRENT WIND CONDITIONS.
......
KIKIIII
(SCREECH)
WHOA !!

WHAT, THEN... THE MONORAIL ...?

THE SUBWAY'S ANOTHER POSSIBIL-ITY.

COGNITION PARTICLES CAN PASS THROUGH CONCRETE AND THE GROUND IF IT'S THIN ENOUGH.

AND IN THAT CASE, WE CAN CHASE IT DOWN!

BUT AS WE SPEAK ...

JIJI

...THE SOURCE IS CIRCLING AROUND AND CHANGING DIRECTIONS.

THAT NARROWS IT DOWN TO A CAR.

GUGU (STOMP)

BUOO (VROOOM)
MOMOKI-SAN!
PLEASE DEPLOY A CHECKPOINT ON BAYSHORE ROAD!

INJECT SAKAIDO.

VUAAA (SHWAAA)

Injection complete.

WHO...
北陸自動車道
HOKURIKU EXPWY
5 西暁
Nishi-Akatsuki
...AM I...?
BUT, PAISEN...
...A CAR IS DISPERSING THE DRIVE TO KILL? DOES THAT MEAN A MURDER TOOK PLACE INSIDE IT?
MAYBE...BUT IT'S POSSIBLE THE MURDER WAS COMMITTED IN ANOTHER LOCATION, AND THE KILLER IS NOW RIDING IN THE CAR.
OR MAYBE THAT VEHICLE WAS USED TO KILL THE VICTIM.
GOTCHA... TO SUM IT UP, WE'RE GOING AFTER EITHER...
...THE SCENE OF THE CRIME...
...THE KILLER, OR THE VICTIM'S... UH, BODY?
OR THE MURDER WEAPON. IT COULD BE ANY ONE OF THOSE, RIGHT?
RIGHT.
BUOOO (VROOM)

FIRST TIME I'VE CHASED DOWN A MOVING SOURCE OF COGNITION PARTICLES ...!
SHE LOOKS HAPPY ...
NEE HEE HEE!
SHE SNICKERED!
検問中

SIGN: CHECKPOINT

OO (WHOOSH)
THAT WAS FAST! LEAVE IT TO THE KURA!

ALL RIGHT!
NOW WE'RE SURE TO CATCH UP!
WAIT A SEC.
DID THE TARGET VEHICLE... JUST VEER AWAY?

THINK THEY NOTICED THE CHECKPOINT AND MADE A DETOUR?
MM...NO, THEY'RE GOING FASTER NOW—
!
IT'S THE HIGHWAY! THEY GOT ON THE HIGHWAY!

OOOO (WHOOSH)
SAKAIDO WILL ARRIVE AT THE CRASH SITE IN ONE MINUTE.

OOO
OKAY, PEOPLE...! AS ALWAYS, LET'S BE THOROUGH.
TOUGOU, YOU'RE ON MACRO-ANALYSIS.
SHIRATAKE, IDENTIFY TIMES AND LOCATIONS.

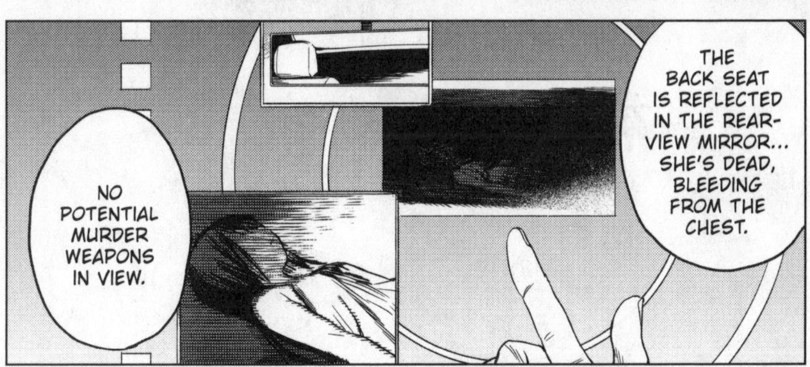

THE LANDSCAPE MATCHES THE REAL SCENERY IN THE TOWN OF NISHI-AKATSUKI, WHICH IS IN FUKUI PREFECTURE.

ヴヴゥ‥ン

VUUN (VUN)

THE YAKITORI RESTAURANT IN THE IMMEDIATE VICINITY EXISTS IN REALITY.

HOWEVER, IT SEEMS THAT IT'S CURRENTLY CLOSED...

...WHILE THE RESTAURANT IN THE ID WELL HAS AN "OPEN" SIGN OUT.

やってます

SIGN: OPEN

VEHICLE MAKE AND MODEL IDENTIFIED.
I'LL REQUEST A LIST OF OWNERS OF THIS MODEL.
IT'S A REAL LUXURY MODEL THAT WENT OUT OF PRODUCTION RECENTLY.
HE'S CLOSING IN ON ANOTHER VEHICLE. NO, MAKE THAT...
BUOOO (VROOOM)
... CRASHING INTO ONE.
DOGGOO (BWAM)
WHOAAAA!!
GYA (SCREECH)
GYA
GYA
BAAAA (HONK)

GOO (VRM)

BAAAAAA

BABBAAAA

北陸 自動車道
HOKURIKU EXPWY
5 西陸
Injecting Sakaido.
Sakaido is awake.
パチ...
PACHI (BLINK)

OKAY, LET'S RUN THROUGH THIS AGAIN.
REMEMBER, THERE'S NO GUARANTEE THAT THINGS WE'VE ALREADY SEEN WILL BE THE SAME FOR THIS SAKAIDO.

Momoki-san!
What is it, Hondou-machi?
THE COGNITION PARTICLES' SOURCE IS NOW HEADING WEST ON THE METROPOLITAN EXPRESSWAY'S BAYSHORE ROUTE.
ゴオオオ
GOOOO (VRM)

Can we close the Metro Expressway temporarily?
...I'LL SEE WHAT I CAN DO.
I'LL ALSO REQUEST ASSISTANCE FROM THE TRAFFIC POLICE AND HIGHWAY PATROL UNIT.

Identify the vehicle that's giving off the cognition particles as quickly as you can.
COPY THAT!

...HOO, BOY... THIS IS INTENSE.
I MEAN, CLOSING THE METRO EXPRESS-WAY?

TOKYO MPD
HMM?
WAIT, ISN'T TODAY ...?

... MOMOKI-SAN.
I'LL TRY TO MAKE AN APPEAL, BUT SEEING AS THERE'S A FOREIGN DIGNITARY ARRIVING IN JAPAN BEFORE NOON TODAY...
...SECURITY ON THE METRO EXPRESSWAY IS ALREADY ON HIGH ALERT.

THE CARS AVOIDING THE ROUTES WHERE TRAFFIC HAS STOPPED THREATEN TO FILL UP EVEN BAYSHORE.
SHUT THAT DOWN TOO, AND WE'LL HAVE COMPLETE AND TOTAL GRIDLOCK.

At this moment... you don't have a full picture of this case, correct?
TRUE.

IF I MAY...
...IS THERE A POSSIBILITY IT'S THE INCEPTION OF A TERRORIST ATTACK?

...WE CAN'T RULE THAT OUT.
THEN THAT MIGHT MAKE THIS EASIER.
KA (TAP)
I'LL HAVE THEM REDIRECT MANPOWER FROM SECURITY.

METROPOLITAN EXPRESSWAY BAYSHORE ROUTE
GOOOO (FWOOSH)

BUOO (VROOOM)
AH-HA-HA! I HEREBY OFFICIALLY DESIGNATE THE TARGET CAR "S"!
"S" AS IN "SERIAL KILLER," "SECRET URGE TO KILL," AND "SPEED"!

ALL RIGHT! NOW WE'LL CATCH UP AND PASS THEM!
DON'T MISS THE VEHICLE GIVING OFF THE PARTICLES THE MOMENT WE OVERTAKE IT, OKAY?

I'LL GIT'ER DONE!

HEH HEH HEH... CAN YOU JUST DO THAT...?
OOO (WHOOSH)
BUT SERIOUSLY, PAISEN—THEY'RE LETTING OUT A RIVER'S WORTH OF COGNITION PARTICLES ON THIS ROAD.
JIJIJI (CRACKLE)
EXACTLY HOW STRONG IS THIS DRIVE TO KILL...?
!?

AHHHH! SHIT! SHIT, SHIT, SHIT!
LAN-GUAGE!
POTTY MOUTH!

"S" IS PULLING AWAY TO THE NORTH!
JIJIJI

GOOOO (VRM)
PAISEN! IT'S THE JUNCTION WE JUST PASSED!
"S" IS HEADED DOWNTOWN VIA OOI JUNCTION!
...
WE'LL EXIT AND DOUBLE BACK AT THE NEXT INTER-CHANGE!

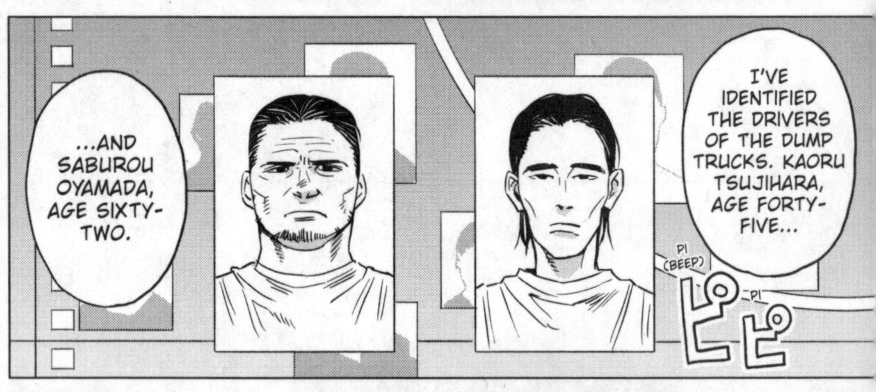
I'VE IDENTIFIED THE DRIVERS OF THE DUMP TRUCKS. KAORU TSUJIHARA, AGE FORTY-FIVE...
PI (BEEP) PI
...AND SABUROU OYAMADA, AGE SIXTY-TWO.

THEY'RE BOTH TRUCK DRIVERS IN REALITY TOO.
THEY WORK FOR SEPARATE COMPANIES LOCATED IN SAITAMA PREFECTURE AND CHIBA PREFECTURE.
NEITHER HAS A CRIMINAL RECORD.
ASK THEIR LOCAL POLICE STATIONS TO VERIFY THEIR SAFETY.

I'VE IDENTIFIED THE DRIVER OF THE STATION WAGON!

THE BACK SEAT REFLECTED IN THE REARVIEW MIRROR...

...WAS DOWN BEFORE... BUT NOW IT'S BEEN FLIPPED UP?

HMM?

FUMINORI TAKEUCHI, THIRTY-TWO YEARS OLD.
PI
HE WAS KILLED IN A TRAFFIC ACCIDENT TWO MONTHS AGO!

SFX: BIKU (FLINCH)

IT WAS HANDLED AS A SINGLE-VEHICLE DISTRACTED DRIVER CRASH... I'LL VERIFY THE DETAILS...
......

Momoki !!

AHEM!
NO NEED TO SHOUT. I CAN HEAR YOU...

...Matsu-
oka-san.

WHAT'S GOING ON!? THE CONNECTION FROM OOI JUNCTION TO THE CENTRAL CIRCULAR ROUTE IS UNDER A TRAFFIC RESTRICTION!

GOO (WHOOSH)

TOKAI JUNCTION IS CLOSED OFF TOO! WE CAN'T FOLLOW THE TRAIL LIKE THIS!

Yeah, it did! So call them off! Or at least get our investigators inside!
THEIR PRIORITY IS JUST TO PREVENT "S" FROM NEARING DOWNTOWN.
BUT AT LEAST WE NOW HAVE MANPOWER FROM THE MPD SECURITY BUREAU.

THOSE GUYS DON'T KNOW ABOUT THE MIZUHANOME OR THE WAKUMUSUBI, DAMMIT!
I'm working with what I've got.

AT THIS POINT IN TIME, YOU DON'T EVEN KNOW WHAT TYPE OF CASE OCCURRED IN "S."
THAT ISN'T ENOUGH TO EASILY PERSUADE ANYONE.

......
I'VE IDENTIFIED THE MAN IN THE SEDAN TOO!
BA (WHIRL)

SADAO TAKAGI, AGE TWENTY-NINE.

PI (BEEP)

LAST MONTH, HE WAS ALSO KILLED IN A SINGLE-VEHICLE DISTRACTED DRIVING ACCIDENT!

DISTRACTED DRIVING...? AWFULLY VAGUE EXPRESSION, THAT...

...BUT IF BOTH OF THE DECEASED APPEARED IN THE ID WELL, IT CAN'T BE MERE COINCIDENCE, CAN IT?

NO SKID MARKS AT THE SCENES OF EITHER CRASH.

WERE THEY BOTH UNCONSCIOUS WHEN THEY CRASHED?

"NO MERE COINCIDENCE" STILL ISN'T ENOUGH REASON.

HERE'S YOUR SMOKING GUN—BOTH CASES WERE ***MURDERS***.

Eh?

I JUST GOT WORD ON THE SCAN OF TAKEUCHI'S WRECK.

WE DETECTED A DRIVE TO KILL THERE.
ZUZUU (ZMM)

IT'S A MIRACLE, SIR.
THE SEIZED VEHICLE WAS STILL IN EVIDENCE.

SFX: JIJI (CRACKLE)

AND...
...THE COGNITION PARTICLES WE FOUND ON IT...

...are from the same drive to kill that Hondoumachi is currently tracking.
ACKNOWL-EDGED.

...THE NEW PARTICLES CREATED AN IDENTICAL ID WELL OF A HIGHWAY OF RUNAWAY VEHICLES.
THE DRIVE TO KILL, FROM THE SAME KILLER, IN TWO SEPARATE PLACES... THIS MAY WELL BE...

......
...a serial murder in progress.

SO... WE HAVE A MURDERER WHO KILLS...
...BY MANIPULATING DRIVERS OR THE CARS THEMSELVES TO CAUSE SINGLE-VEHICLE ACCIDENTS?

OOO (WHOOSH)
All the more reason we can't let them near downtown.
However, I'll deploy a checkpoint by the Yamate Tunnel exit.
CIRCULAR ROUTE NUMBER 8
......
CAN YOU BLOCK OFF OOHASHI JUNCTION?

...CARS ON ITS INBOUND ROUTE ARE BEING EXAMINED.

SO WE'RE ALL GOOD AS LONG AS WE STAY AWAY FROM DOWNTOWN? ...WELL, LET'S NOT WORRY ABOUT THAT.
THE WAY IT LOOKS NOW, WE MIGHT BE ABLE TO CATCH UP TO "S" LIKE YOU PREDICTED, PAISEN.

FROM WHAT WE KNOW, BOTH FUMINORI TAKEUCHI AND SADAO TAKAGI CRASHED ON THE TOKYO-NAGOYA EXPRESSWAY'S OUTBOUND ROUTE...
IF THAT CONNECTION MEANS SOMETHING...
...THEN "S" WILL HEAD FOR THE SAME PLACE...

GOOOO (VRM)

CENTRAL CIRCULAR ROUTE

THIS IS MATSUOKA! WE'RE INSIDE YAMATE TUNNEL.

OO (WHOOSH)

LOOKS LIKE "S" GOT ON THE TOKYO-NAGOYA EXPRESSWAY AT OOHASHI JUNCTION! ITS DIRECTION IS...

DOGOO (KABOOM)

Sakaido has died!

SAKAIDO HAS ALREADY DIED FOUR TIMES...

...AND THIS TIME, HE DIDN'T EVEN NOTICE KAERU'S BODY...

I DON'T HAVE ENOUGH INFORMATION TO MAKE MANY DEDUCTIONS.

HELL... WHAT IS THE MYSTERY OF KAERU'S DEATH?

I CAN'T EVEN SEE THE GENERAL OUTLINES OF IT YET...!

Injecting Sakaido!

OOO (WHOOSH)

TOKYO-NAGOYA EXPRESSWAY, OUTBOUND ROUTE

AWWW YEAH! NOW WE'RE ON THE TOMEI!

HOW'S IT LOOK!? DID WE PASS THE TARGET?

AARGH, WE WERE SO CLOSE! NOT THAT I KNOW THAT FOR SURE, BUT...

...THEY'RE AHEAD OF US AGAIN.

TAKE YOUR TIME! WE'LL SPEED UP AND LOCATE IT!

JIJI (CRACKLE)
JI
REAL CLOSE NOW...!
I'M GOING TO CASUALLY PASS "S."
OOO (WHOOSH)
GET A GOOD LOOK AT THE VEHICLE'S INTERIOR, THE DRIVER'S FACE, ANYTHING LIKE THAT.
YES, MA'AM!
BUOO (VROOOM)
......!
OOO

HUH?
THAT'S ...!
DIRECTOR!
LOOK IN THE CAR THAT'S APPEARED BEHIND SAKAIDO ...!
!?
HONDOU-MACHI!
"S" IS AWARE OF YOU TWO!
THAT MEANS ...!

"S" must be at the scene right now.
WHAT !?
GYO (JOLT)
PAISEN, BREAK THIS DOWN FOR ME!?
OOOO (WHOOSH)
"S" ISN'T A CAR THAT'S GOING TO CRASH? IS THE KILLER ACTUALLY BEHIND THE WHEEL...!?

SO THE ACCIDENT-IN-WAITING IS SOMEWHERE ELSE, THEN ...!?
COGNITION PARTICLES FOR THE DRIVE TO KILL APPEAR WHEN A HOMICIDAL ACTION ACTUALLY TAKES PLACE.
THAT IS TO SAY, THE CRIME ITSELF SHOULD HAVE ALREADY BEEN COMMITTED.
THERE'VE BEEN NO REPORTS OF A CRASH ON THE TOMEI EXPRESSWAY... BUT ONE EXPLANATION COULD BE...

...THAT OUR KILLER INSTALLED SOME KIND OF CRASH-CAUSING DEVICE ON THE VICTIM'S VEHICLE...
...AND THEY'RE NOW DRIVING ALONGSIDE THAT CAR IN ORDER TO MAKE SURE THE CRASH HAPPENS...
BUOOOO (VROOOM)
Inspector Hondou-machi!

This is Kitano from Highway Patrol. We're here to assist.

We await your orders.

......

I WANT YOU TO STOP ALL CARS UP TO ONE KILOMETER AHEAD OF OUR POSITION.

OUR MURDER SUSPECT IS AMONG THESE CARS. THERE'S NO TELLING WHAT THEY'LL DO IF WE SPOOK THEM.

...! COPY THAT.

WAIT! ALSO...

SA (SWUP)

...DON'T USE YOUR SIREN. STAY UNDER THE RADAR AS YOU PULL AHEAD.

......

Yes, ma'am!

PHEW... THIS IS A BIG RELIEF...

EVEN "S" CAN'T POSSIBLY CAUSE AN ACCIDENT WHEN ALL THE CARS ARE STOPPED, RIGHT?
ブオォォォ
BUOOOO (VROOOM)
I WOULDN'T BE SO SURE.
WE STILL DON'T KNOW HOW "S" IS MAKING DEADLY ACCIDENTS HAPPEN.

IF WE DON'T KNOW THEIR M.O., IT'S TOO SOON TO RELAX.
...

SFX: JIJI (CRACKLE)
!

PAISEN!

WE PASSED "S"...!?

KIKIII (SCREECH)

BAN (BAM)

THEY RAN...?
BUT WHERE !?
EBINA BRIDGE
EBINA BRIDGE
OO (WHOOSH)
THE EBINA SERVICE AREA...!
SHOOT! THEY GOT OFF AT ANOTHER JUNCTION ...!
OO

OOO

!

GASA (FWISH)

BA (SHWIP)

BA

I'M CLOSE ...!

DO
DO
DO
DO
(MENACE)
DA
(DASH)
FUKUSEN-KUN! IT'S THE WHITE CAR NEAR THE MIDDLE!
A WHITE CAR!? YOU GOTTA GIVE ME MORE THAN THAT...!
WHERE IS IT!?
BAN
(SLAM)
DON'T APPROACH UNPRE-PARED!
DON'T WORRY!
SUCHA
(CLACK)
PAISEN! ISN'T THE KILLER THERE!?

My own senpai taught me well!
DON'T YOU DARE, HONDOU-MACHI!
STAND BY!
WAIT FOR BACK-UP!

SERIAL MURDERS...
SINGLE-VEHICLE ACCIDENTS...

ズズ...
ZUZU (ZMM)
A HOMICIDAL ACTION THAT'S ALREADY TAKEN PLACE...

WHAT'S THE M.O...!?
Do you hear me, Hondou-machi!?

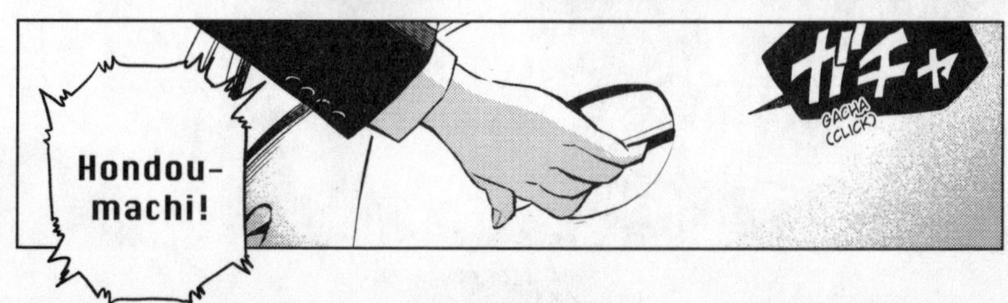
ガチャ
GACHA (CLICK)
Hondou-machi!

DO (WHAM)

KAERU-CHAN...

OOO (WHOOSH)

GYA (SCREECH)

GYA

BAAAA (HONK)

BA

BAAAA

DON (SLAM)

Sakaido has died!

END

ドルルンー

DORURUN (BRRM)

!!

PAISEN !?

DO (WHAM)
DO
DOO
...!
DAMMIT!
WE HAVE INJURED BYSTANDERS!
DOKA (CRUNCH)
PLEASE SEND AN AMBULANCE!

DA (DASH)

OOOOO (WHOOSH)

BA (FWIP)

FREEZE!

STEP OUT OF THE CAR WITH YOUR HANDS IN THE AIR! NOW!

GIRI (GRIT)

BUO (VOOSH)

GASSHAA (SHATTER)

ZZZ...
ZZZ...

スピー…
SUPIII (SNOOZE)
HE'S ASLEEP !?

......
クン
KUN
クン
KUN (SNIFF)
WHAT'S THAT SWEET SMELL ...?

THE PASSENGER SIDE DOOR WAS UNLOCKED ...?

GACHA (CHAK)
PAISEN!
YOU OKAY!?

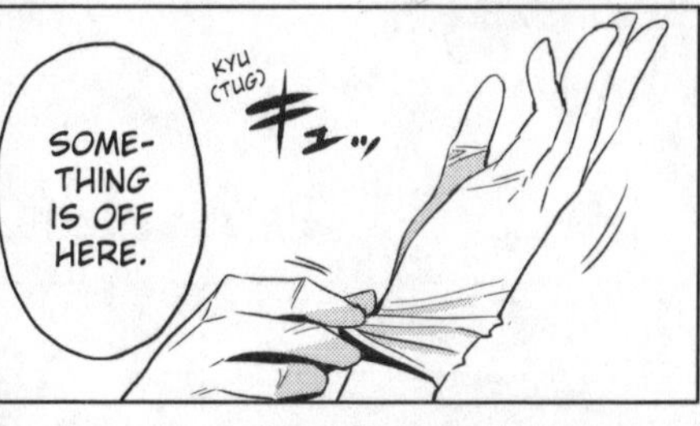
KYU (TUG)
SOME-THING IS OFF HERE.

I bagged a cup from the vehicle.
I'll send it to forensics.
UNDER-STOOD.

IT'S POSSIBLE THIS DRIVER WAS DRUGGED WITH SOMETHING, MAYBE SLEEP MEDICATION.

NO VISIBLE WOUNDS ON THE DRIVER...
YUSA (SHAKE)
YUSA
HEY, BUDDY, RISE AND SHINE!

GOTTA GET IN HERE. PARDON ME...

GOSO

GOSO (RUMMAGE)

OH-HO!

FOUND HIS DRIVER'S LICENSE.

HE'S RYOUHEI HASHIMOTO, FORTY-TWO YEARS OLD.

His address is in Tokyo. Odaiba, Minato Ward...

I HAVE A MATCH IN THE ID WELL.

WHILE SAKAIDO ISN'T AWARE OF HIM, HE'S BEHIND THE WHEEL OF ONE OF THE REAR CARS.

THE REAL RYOUHEI HASHIMOTO WORKS FOR A FILM COMPANY.

THEIR ADDRESS IS ALSO IN ODAIBA.

ODAIBA...

TSUJI-HARA AND OYAMADA'S TRUCKS...
PI PI (BEEP)
...WERE BOTH BOUND FOR ODAIBA THIS MORNING, CARRYING CARGO TO A SHIPPING COMPANY.
USING THE FOOTAGE FROM THEIR DASHBOARD CAMERAS...

...I FOUND A LINK.
ALL THREE STOPPED AT A CONVENIENCE STORE ALONG BAYSHORE ROAD.

THIS CAR HAS NO DASHCAM... BUT WE CAN CHECK SECURITY CAMERA FOOTAGE.

WE'RE LOOKING FOR VEHICLES THAT ENTERED THE SERVICE AREA AFTER WE STARTED STOPPING CARS. I COUNT...

...THREE CARS, INCLUDING "S"!
THEN THE KILLER ...!
!
THEY MUST HAVE FOLLOWED "S" TO WATCH THE ACCIDENT, RIGHT!?
OKAY... WHAT TYPES!?

I'm sending you their locations.
GOT THEM!
PAISEN!
HE NEEDS MEDICAL ATTENTION.

OKAY, I'LL TAKE RED!

THEN I'LL TAKE BLACK!
BE CAREFUL!

OH, WAIT!
CHA (CLACK)
WANT THIS?

I'M NOT GONNA GO DO ANYTHING CRAZY LIKE YOU, PAISEN!

...UM.
THAT'D BE MULTIPLE CODE VIOLATIONS... I'M GOOD.

CHIKA (CLICK)
CAPTAIN KITANO?

Please expand your blockade to cover the Ebina Service Area exit.
COPY THAT.

HEY. LET'S ROLL.
BURON (VROOM)
YES, SIR!

THAT SHOULD BLOCK OFF THE KILLER'S ESCAPE ROUTE...!
PI (BIP)

TA (TMP)
TA

TO (TAP)

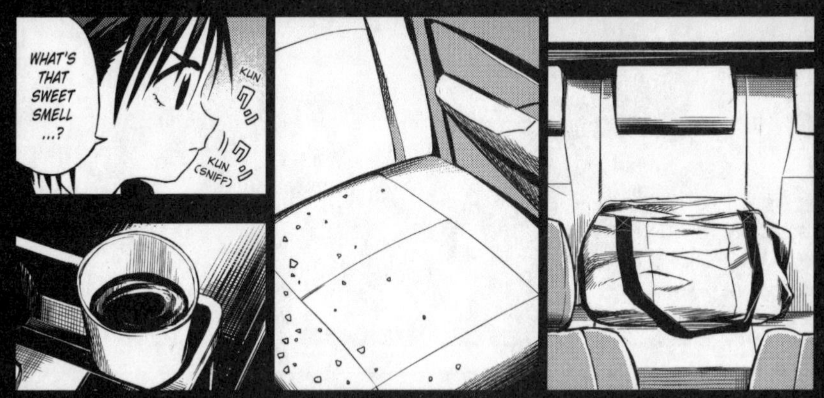
WHAT'S THAT SWEET SMELL ...?
KUN
KUN (SNIFF)

......!?
Matsuoka-san!
OO (WHOOSH)
WHAT !?
JIJI (CRACKLE)
PLEASE CHECK THE PASSENGER SIDE OF TAKEUCHI'S VEHICLE FOR TRACES OF BLOOD!
JI
JI
JI

SHE'S RIGHT...

THERE'S A LARGE BLOODSTAIN ON THE PASSENGER SIDE SEAT.
WOULDN'T MAKE MUCH SENSE FOR THAT PATTERN TO HAVE COME FROM THE DRIVER.

...!?
WHAT DOES THAT MEAN?

...IT'S THE KILLER.

THEY WEREN'T WATCHING FOR "S" TO CRASH FROM ANOTHER VEHICLE.
THEY WERE RIDING IN THE SAME CAR.

SU (SWUP)
That can't be...
We're talking about crashes that killed the drivers!

THE KILLER COULDN'T HAVE WALKED AWAY FROM THEM UN-HARMED!
IN FACT, DOESN'T THIS MEAN THEY WERE ACTUALLY INJURED IN TAKEUCHI'S CRASH!?

I KNOW. AND THEY WERE PROBABLY INJURED IN TAKAGI'S CRASH TOO.
BUT IF THERE'S NO SECOND CORPSE, THEY MUST HAVE SURVIVED.

スルリ
SURURI (SWIP)

AND NOW THEIR THIRD CRASH KILLING HAS FAILED...
...SADLY FOR THEM.

GOT THE SECURITY CAMERA FOOTAGE.

SOMEONE EXITED "S" FROM THE PASSENGER SIDE.
IT'S A WOMAN.

TRACE HER MOVE-MENT.

I'M WORKING ON IT...
...BUT THE SECURITY CAMERAS IN THE AREA ARE TOO FEW AND FAR BETWEEN...

TAKEUCHI WAS TWO MONTHS AGO.

TAKAGI WAS ONE MONTH AGO...

THE KILLER'S BEEN DOING THIS ONCE A MONTH, EVEN WHILE INJURED...
WOULD SHE REALLY GIVE UP THIS EASILY...?

SO THEN...
...WE WERE CHASING THE CRIME SCENE, THE WEAPON, THE KILLER, AND THE VICTIM ALL AT ONCE...?
NO COGNITION PARTICLES DETECTED ON THE BLACK CAR.
IF IT WAS THE KILLER'S CAR, THERE'D BE SOME, RIGHT?
SO WHY IS THERE NOTHING EVEN WHEN I EXPAND THE DETECTION RADIUS TO THE ENTIRE SERVICE AREA...!?

CRAP...THE KILLER IS MOVING TOO QUICKLY!
SHE SWITCHED VEHICLES IMMEDIATELY AFTER EXITING "S."

IT'S A BUS!
SHE SLIPPED INTO A GROUP ON A TOUR BUS!

I'M INCREASING MY WAKU-MUSUBI'S SENSITIVI-TY...
...TO SEARCH FARTHER OUTSIDE THE SERVICE AREA...
KACHI (CLICK)
カチ
カチ
KACHI
カチ
KACHI
カチ
KACHI

カチ
KACHI
カチ
KACHI
カチ
KACHI
カチ
KACHI

ジジ…
JIJI (CRACKLE)
ジジジ…
JIJIJI

THE KILLER IS ON THE MOVE!

DORUN (REV)
ドルンッ
I'M IN PURSUIT!

GOOOOOO (VRM)

WHAT THE HELL, PAISEN ...!?
WHAT DOES SHE THINK SHE'S DOING!? THAT'S A WRECK! AND EVIDENCE!
NO WAY!

I AM SO SORRY! URGENT POLICE CHASE!
SHUBA (ZOOM)
HEY! GET BACK HERE!

BAN (SLAM)

HEY, PAISEN !?
It's fine. I parked "S" at the exit!
HUH!?

ブォォォォ
BUOOOO (VROOOM)

IT SEEMS THAT THE KILLER IS ATTEMPTING SOMETHING IN THE VEIN OF AN... UNPROVOKED MURDER-SUICIDE.
SHE HITCHES RIDES ON LONG-HAUL TRUCKS AND SLIPS DRUGS TO THEIR DRIVERS TO CLOUD THEIR MINDS. AND FOR SOME REASON, SHE HAS A FIXATION ABOUT CARRYING IT OUT ON THE TOMEI EXPRESSWAY...

THE REASON THE CRASHES END UP AS ONLY SINGLE-VEHICLE ACCIDENTS COULD BE THAT THE KILLER HERSELF TAKES CONTROL OF THE STEERING WHEEL FROM THE PASSENGER SEAT.
......!
THEN, EVEN WHILE SERIOUSLY INJURED, SHE ERASES ALL EVIDENCE THAT SHE WAS THERE...
...REMOVES THE DASHCAM, AND LEAVES THE SITE OF THE CRASH.

SINCE THE CRASHES OCCUR ON AN EXPRESSWAY, AS LONG AS THE WRECK DOESN'T BLOCK THE ROAD, THE PASSING CARS WILL DRIVE PAST RATHER THAN STOP AND RUBBERNECK.
IS THAT WHY THERE WERE BARELY ANY WITNESS STATEMENTS ABOUT A WOMAN ESCAPING THE CRASHED CARS...?

I'VE IDENTIFIED THE TOUR BUS!
CONTACT ITS DRIVER.
Ah! Please do so carefully.

THE KILLER COULD BE SEATED NEAR THE DRIVER, WAITING FOR HER CHANCE TO DRUG THEM.
OOOO (WHOOSH)
SO IF SHE'S WATCHING THE DRIVER FROM NEARBY, SHE COULD CATCH ON. IF SHE JUMPS INTO ACTION...

...there will be many victims.
WHAT DO WE DO, THEN?
GOO (VRM)
HONDOUMACHI, I HOPE YOU AREN'T GETTING ANY FUNNY IDEAS!
FOUND IT.

GOOOOO (VRRM)

TAKE US CLOSER, PLEASE.

WHAT'S YOUR PLAN?

SINCE WE CAN'T RISK ROUSING THE KILLER'S SUSPICION...
...I'LL HAVE TO RESORT TO SLIGHTLY DRASTIC MEASURES.

Momoki-san, do we have a visual on the killer's face yet?
NOT YET... BUT...

OOOO (WHOOSH)
...WE'RE CURRENTLY VERIFYING THE OTHER PASSENGERS' FACES...
...USING A BUS THAT'S APPEARED IN THE ID WELL.
I DON'T EVEN KNOW MY OWN NAME...
...BUT I DO KNOW...
...THE RESULTS OF AN EXPERIMENT STUDYING THE EFFECTS OF WIND FROM PASSING TRAINS ON PEOPLE STANDING ON THE PLATFORM.
THEY COULD REMAIN STANDING STRAIGHT IN THE FACE OF WINDS TRAVELING TEN METERS PER SECOND.
AT FIFTEEN M/S, PEOPLE BECOME UNSTEADY.
AT TWENTY, THEY HAVE TO BEND FORWARD.
AT TWENTY-FIVE, IT BECOMES DIFFICULT TO FREELY CHANGE POSITION.
AT THIRTY, WHILE LEANING FORWARD AS FAR AS THEY CAN, THEY HAVE TO KEEP SHIFTING THEIR WEIGHT FORWARD TO REMAIN STANDING.
AT THIRTY-FIVE, THEY'LL BE BLOWN AWAY NO MATTER WHAT THEY DO.

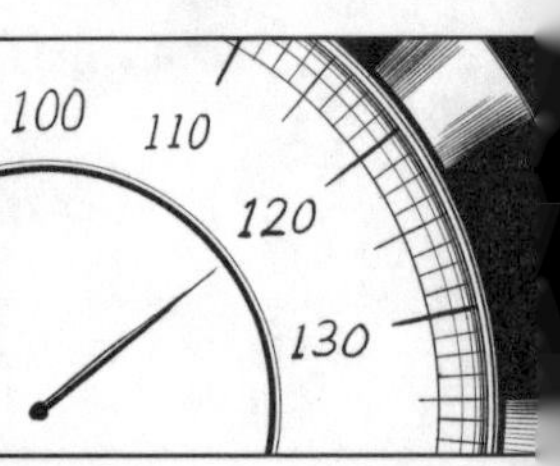

GOOOOOO (VRM)
HUP!
HUP!
HUP!
HUP!
TO (THUMP)
TO
TO
TO
GA

OOOOO (WHOOSH)
SHOULD WE SPEED UP TOO!?
THAT'D DEFEAT THE WHOLE POINT! DON'T WORRY. HOLD THIS SPEED!
GASHI (GRAB)
COME ON, THIS WAY!
GOOOO
WE'LL NEVER MAKE IT IN TIME!
DON'T GIVE UP!
TRUST ME AND HOLD OUT YOUR HAND!
I PROMISE YOU I'LL TAKE IT!
HUH!?
WHOA, WHAT ARE YOU—
GA (GRIP)

GOAAAAAAAA
(VWOOSH)
KEEP IT UP A LITTLE LONGER, TINA!
THIS IS THE LAST ONE!
DAAAMN! MAN, YOU'RE BADASS!
OOO
(WHOO)
NOW YOU!
BA
(FWIP)

OOOO
...GOING AFTER MY CAR...!
NO. I'M...
......!
BA
GOOOO (VRM)
GA (GRAB)
The faces of the id well passengers match the tour group roster.

PI PI PI PI PI PI PI PI PI (BEEP)

ID WELLS ARE THE WORLD AS SEEN BY A KILLER. IN SOME CASES, THAT WORLD CONTAINS THE KILLER THEMSELF.

BUOOO (VROOM)
NU (LEAN)
!!?
HEY! WHAT THE HELL ARE YOU THINKING !?
GU (PRESS)
DON'T PANIC!
ZURU (SLIDE)
......
KEEP GOING SLOWLY, JUST LIKE THAT!
TRY NOT TO LET THEM NOTICE US!
IS SHE OUT OF HER MIND...?

I'VE HAD IT UP TO HERE WITH YOUR CRAP, HONDOU-MACHI!

GOOOOO (VRM)

GOOD, GOOD.

—IS WHAT I CAN ALMOST HEAR MATSUOKA-SAN YELLING NOW...

KEEP IT UP. STEADY NOW...

OOO (WHOO)

MOMOKI-SAN.

Please tell the bus driver to ignore their emergency exit sign.

HUH?

UH, SURE. WILL DO... BUT...

WHAT ON EARTH ARE YOU PLANNING TO DO...?

BUOOO
(VROOOM)
ISN'T THIS A BIT TOO MUCH BACK-TO-BACK INSANITY...!?
GOOOO

DA (DASH)
BAN (BAM)
OOOO (WHOOSH)
...I REMEMBER WHO I AM...
...WHEN I SEE THAT DEAD GIRL...
... KAËRU-CHAN.

BI (VREEE)
MY NAME IS SAKAIDO ...
NO TIME FOR A MONO-LOGUE!
BA (LEAP)
... CRAP!
GYUAAA (SWERVE)
GYA (SCREECH)
GYA
GYA

DOGGOO
(KABOOM)
OOO
(WHOOSH)
GAKIN
(CLANG)
GURAA
(TILT)
GYA
(SCREECH)
GYA
GYA
GYA

BAUN (BWOM)
!?
WHOA-AAA—
GUOOO (LOOM)
OHH!?
DO (WHAM)

GOO (WHOOM)
GA (GRRK)
GA
GA
GA
...!!
GUN (LURCH)
DODOO (BADOOM)

BUOOO (VROOOM)

GOGON (BABAM)

GOO (WHOM)

GAKO (KACHUNK)

YET, IT WAS FLIPPED UP WHEN I FOUND IT...
DOES THAT MEAN THE KILLER RAISED IT?
AND THEN FLED THE SCENE BEFORE I REGAINED CONSCIOUS-NESS?

HUH? NO, THAT'S NOT RIGHT...
THE SEAT WAS DOWN FOR SOME TIME EVEN AFTER SAKAIDO STARTED DRIVING.

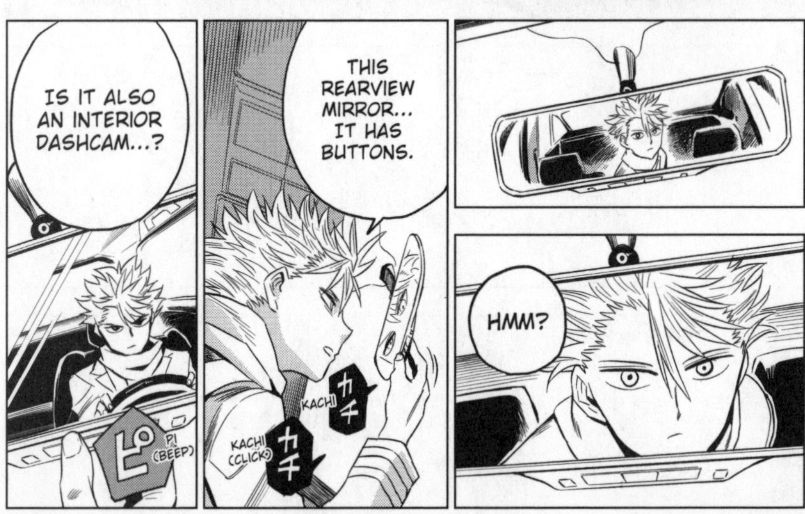
THIS REARVIEW MIRROR... IT HAS BUTTONS.
カチ KACHI
カチ KACHI (CLICK)
IS IT ALSO AN INTERIOR DASHCAM...?
ピ PI (BEEP)
HMM?

HEH... LOOKS LIKE ALL THE MEMORIES I COULD ASK FOR ARE RIGHT HERE.

......
...WHAT'S GOING ON HERE?

REPLAY
SO WHAT EXACTLY HAPPENED ...?

THE BACK SEAT WAS OPEN... BUT...
...WHEN I GOT ON THE EXPRESSWAY, IT IMMEDIATELY SHUT.
WHAT KIND OF FORCE RETURNED THE BACKREST TO AN UPRIGHT POSITION?

FOR A SPLIT SECOND, SOMETHING CROSSES THE SCREEN...

THIS IS...

SOMETHING CRASHING INTO THE REAR SIDE OF THE BACKREST.

SOMETHING FELL...
...THROUGH THIS SUNROOF...

I'VE CRACKED THE CASE.
END

#04 REVERSAL

...DIRECTLY BEFORE SOMETHING FALLS THROUGH THE SUNROOF...

...FOR A SPLIT SECOND, AS SAKAIDO IS ABOUT TO MERGE ONTO THE HIGHWAY FROM THE ACCELERATION LANE...
...THE DASHCAM CAPTURES THE SHADOW OF A LONG-HAIRED WOMAN IN THE SMOKE.

HER HEIGHT... SEEMS TO BE A GOOD MATCH TO KAERU'S.

WHAT'S MORE, THE ON-RAMP CONNECTING THE TOLL AREA TO THE EXPRESSWAY SHOULD BE OFF-LIMITS TO PEDESTRIANS.
FOR SOMEONE TO IGNORE THAT AND ENTER ANYWAY...

...THEY WOULD NEED TO HAVE A POWERFUL REASON.
WHAT IF KAERU KNEW THE NATURE OF THIS ID WELL'S WORLD, AND WENT AFTER SAKAIDO'S CAR...
...TO TRY AND STOP ME...?

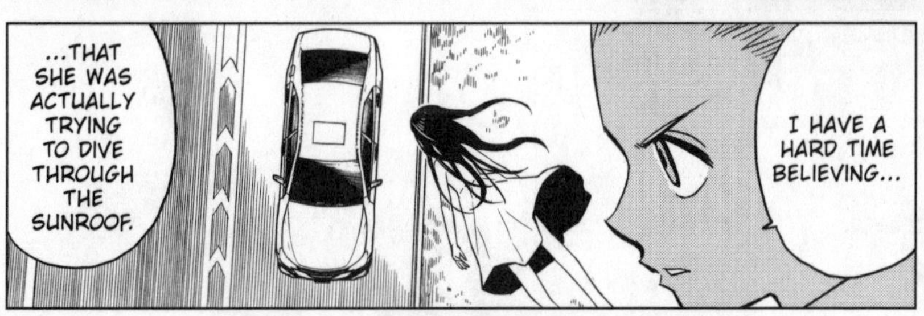
I HAVE A HARD TIME BELIEVING...
...THAT SHE WAS ACTUALLY TRYING TO DIVE THROUGH THE SUNROOF.

MY THEORY IS THAT SHE INTENDED TO STOP SAKAIDO...
...BEFORE HIS VEHICLE COULD MERGE ONTO THE EXPRESSWAY.

THAT'S RIGHT...
I DID USE THE BRAKES— ON THE ON-RAMP'S CURVE.

IT WAS THE LAST CHANCE BEFORE HE GOT ON...

KIKIIIIII (SCREECH)

IF SAKAIDO HAD FOUND KAERU THEN, HE SURELY WOULD HAVE PARKED AT ONCE.

BUT THE ID WELL KILLED KAERU.
TO PURSUE THE DUMP TRUCKS THAT CAREENED THROUGH THE INJURED PEOPLE AT THE CRASH SITE...
...SAKAIDO ACCELERATED EARLY. THAT'S HOW KAERU ENDED UP PLUNGING THROUGH THE SUNROOF.

?
IF YOU'RE CORRECT, WOULDN'T THAT HAVE BEEN A LUCKY BREAK FOR KAERU?
IT WOULD HAVE, EXCEPT ...
...PEOPLE KEEP ALL SORTS OF THINGS IN THEIR CAR'S TRUNKS, DON'T THEY?

BERI (PEEL) べり…
SO IT WAS THIS...

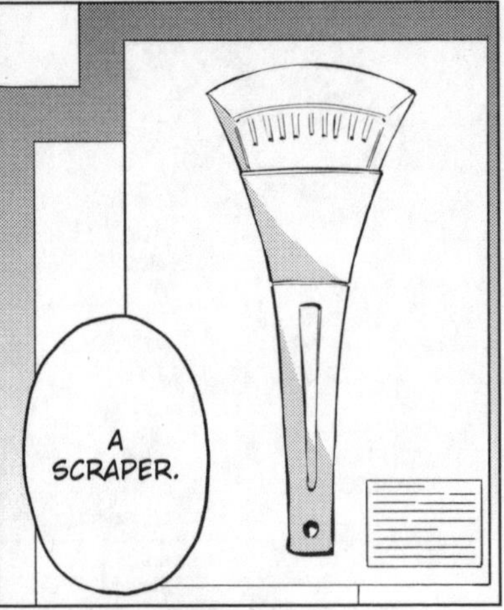
A SCRAPER.

A SCRAPER?
AH, YOU MEAN FOR REMOVING ICE FROM THE WINDOWS IN WINTER?

THE VERY SAME.
WHEN KAERU PLUMMETED THROUGH THE SUNROOF...

...SAKAIDO'S CAR WAS RUNNING OVER DEBRIS FROM THE WRECKS, SO HE COULDN'T FEEL THE IMPACT.
ALSO, THANKS TO THE EXPLOSIVE SOUND OF THE TRUCKS IN FRONT OF HIM PLOWING THROUGH ANOTHER WRECK...

FINALLY, WHEN KAERU HIT THE LOWERED BACKREST AND BOUNCED INTO THE TRUNK...

...HE DIDN'T HEAR KAERU'S PLUNGE INTO THE REAR SEAT EITHER.

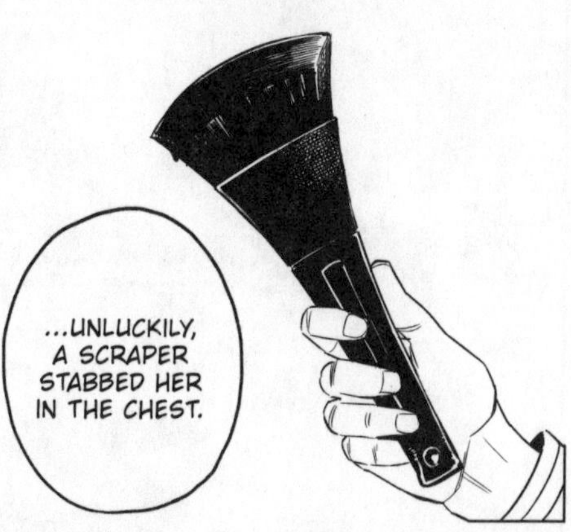
...UNLUCKILY, A SCRAPER STABBED HER IN THE CHEST.

BUT THEY'RE MOSTLY RUBBER...!

...IT PROBABLY HAD METAL PARTS HOLDING IT TOGETHER.

WHY...?

OOO (WHOOSH)
FOR ME...?

DID YOU DIE...
...TO SAVE ME...!?

STAY SHARP. WE STILL HAVEN'T SOLVED THE REAL-WORLD CASE.

SHIRATAKE. HABUTAE. BACK TO YOUR JOBS.

AH! YES, SIR!

WAKASHIKA, DON'T YOU RELAX YET EITHER.

YES, SIR!

KOHARU-CHAN SHOULD BE ABOUT TO MAKE CONTACT WITH THE KILLER NOW.

WE NEED THAT I.D. FAST.

Koharu-chan, don't overdo it.

GOOO (VRM)

I'M NOT OVERDOING IT OR ACTING CRAZY.

OOOO (WHOOSH)
I'M ONLY DOING WHAT'S WITHIN THE BOUNDS OF MY ABILITY...!
GASSHA (SMASH)
HFF!
HFF!
HFF!
BADGE: METROPOLITAN POLICE DEPARTMENT
HFF!
HFF!
HEY! FUKUSEN!
HFFFFFF!
POLICE
OOO

Matsu-oka-san!?
YOU'RE STUCK CHASING AFTER HONDOU-MACHI, RIGHT?
OH, UH, YES, SIR!
DON'T YOU GO NUTS TOO.
KEEP A GOOD DISTANCE.

HUH!? BUT I HAVE TO HELP HER...!
SHE'S DOING SOMETHING CRAZY RIGHT NOW...
All you need to do is brace for trouble—don't get yourself dragged into it.
...!?

...SHOULD WE AT LEAST KEEP AN EYE ON THEM FROM NEARBY?
YOU THINK BABYSITTING IS PART OF OUR JOB DESCRIPTION?
...
BACK TO WORK.

THIS IS JUST TYING UP LOOSE ENDS, BUT TO COVER ALL OUR BASES...
THE TWO VEHICLES THAT ENTERED THE SERVICE AREA WITH HASHIMOTO'S CAR, "S"...
..."RED" AND "BLACK"—IT LOOKS LIKE THEY WERE BOTH CLOSE TO "S" FOR THE ENTIRE DRIVE FROM ODAIBA.

NOW, WAS IT ONLY COINCIDENCE THAT ALL THREE CARS ENTERED THE SERVICE AREA AT THE SAME TIME...?
......
"RED"... IS GONE.
Matsu-oka-san.
HOW ABOUT "BLACK" !?

We were... unable to locate the vehicle from the report.
BOTH OF THEM VANISHED ...!?
CLUNK

ゴォォォォ
GOOOOOO (VRM)

AH HA HA!

'SCUSE ME, COMING THROUGH!

SHHHH!

......
ISN'T IT STILL MOVING?

WHAT'S GOING ON? SOME KIND OF ON-BOARD ENTERTAIN-MENT?
HISO HISO (WHISPER)
HUH!?
UH...YES, MA'AM, YOU HIT THE NAIL ON THE HEAD! IT'S A LITTLE SURPRISE.

I THOUGHT THIS ONLY HAPPENED IN MOVIES!
CHA (CLACK)

OH, WHAT FUN!
SHHHH!
KEEP IT DOWN!

MY! HOW DASHING!
TEE HEE HEE!
HEE HEE HEE!
SHE LOOKS GOOD IN A UNIFORM BECAUSE SHE'S SO YOUNG.
AH HA HA!
OH, YOU!

......

WHAT THE—?

WHO ARE YOU!?

I'M WITH THE POLICE.

HUH? ...SO YOU'RE THE ONE WHO TRIPPED THE EMERGENCY EXIT ALARM ...!?

THANKS FOR YOUR COOPERATION.

DID ANY SUSPICIOUS PEOPLE BOARD THIS BUS AT THE EBINA SERVICE AREA!?

I COULDN'T ELIMINATE ANYONE...!

HUH?

SU
(SWIP)

JIJI
(CRACKLE)
JI

GASA
(RUSTLE)

ZA
(SHFF)

!

Momoki-san!
The woman who slipped into the tour group—did she get back off the bus before it left?

VAAAN
(BAM)

SHE'S RIGHT!
SHIT!

WE'VE BEEN HAD...!

IT'S THE SAME WOMAN WITH A DIFFERENT OUTFIT AND HAIRSTYLE!
NOW WAIT A MINUTE ...
DOESN'T THIS MEAN THE KILLER KNEW LEAVING HER CLOTHES ON AN UNRELATED BUS WOULD THROW OUR INVESTIGATION INTO CONFUSION?

THESE ACTIONS... ONLY MAKE SENSE IF THE KILLER KNOWS ABOUT THE WAKUMUSUBI ...!!

Not yet...

I HAVEN'T CRACKED THIS CASE YET...!

THIS DEDUCTION DOESN'T ADD UP.

HUH?

WHAT DID HE JUST SAY...!?

...OH!

THERE'S NO BLOOD ON THE OTHER SIDE.
KURU (FLIP) クルッ

OO (WHOOSH)
IN OTHER WORDS, THIS ICE SCRAPER ONLY JUST SO HAPPENED TO BE HERE.
IT DIDN'T STAB KAERU-CHAN'S CHEST.

THEN WHO WAS THE WOMAN ON THE OVERPASS?
AND WHAT ABOUT THE SHADOW THAT PASSED THROUGH THE SUNROOF...?

ALSO, THAT THEORY WOULDN'T EXPLAIN THE LARGE BLOODSTAIN ON MY BACK...
THERE ARE EVEN MORE UNKNOWN FACTORS NOW... BUT THAT'S ALL RIGHT.

GOOOOO (VRM)
AS LONG AS I, THE BRILLIANT DETECTIVE, AM HERE...
...THIS WORLD IS IN GOOD HANDS.

......

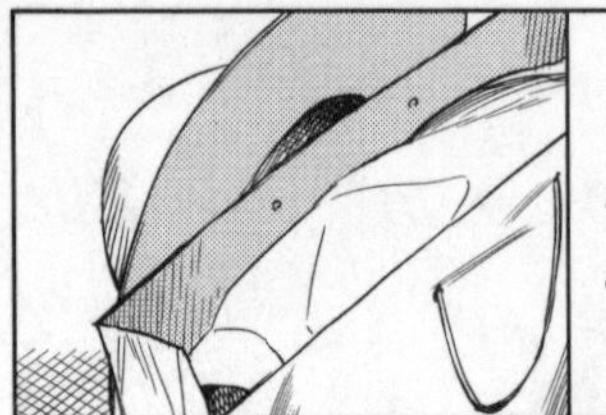
PLAYING A TRICK LIKE THIS... TO THROW US OFF HER TRAIL...

WAS HER GOAL TO ESCAPE THE SERVICE AREA UNDE-TECTED?

SO SHE CAN DRUG A DIFFERENT VICTIM ON A DIFFERENT DAY...
...GET BACK ON THE TOMEI, AND REDO THIS ARBITRARY MURDER-SUICIDE...?
...NO.

THIS KILLER...
...WOULDN'T LEAVE A JOB UNFINISHED.

THIS KILLER... WANTS TO BE INVOLVED IN THESE ACCIDENTS TO THE LAST.

SHE WANTS TO BE RIGHT AT THE CRASH SCENE.

PARDON ME!
BA (WHOOSH)
GARA (RATTLE)
GOOOO (VRM)
OOOO (WHOOSH)
DO YOU WANT TO STOP THE BUS AND RETURN TO THE CAR!?
JIJI (CRACKLE)

JIJIJI
...!?
JI
ANOTHER READING ON THE WAKUMUSUBI ...!?
AND IT'S COMING CLOSER ...!
FUKU-SEN-KUN!
OOOO
HUH !?
WHAT'S SHE TELLING ME...?
THE WAKUMUSUBI?
SU (SHWIP)

DO
(BADUM)
SO THIS IS THAT WEIRD DEVICE ...?
DO
DO
DO

DO
DO
DO
DO
BIII
BIII
(BREEP)
751846
DETECTION

...!?
GYURURURURU (SWERVE)
!
BUOOO (VROOM)
KYU
KYU
KYU (SCREECH)

GUOOOO (VOOSH)

OOOO (WHOOSH)

WHAT THE—

WHAT'S GOING ON!?

DO
(CRUNCH)

OOO (WHOOSH)

GOOOOO (VRM)

IF THERE'S A BRILLIANT DETECTIVE...

...THEN THERE'S A MEANING TO EVERY-THING.

EVERY-THING...

...IS CON-NECTED.

END

TRANSLATION NOTES

COMMON HONORIFICS

no honorific: Indicates familiarity or closeness; if used without permission, addressing someone in this manner would constitute an insult.

-san: The Japanese equivalent of Mr./Mrs./Miss. If a situation calls for politeness, this is the fail-safe honorific.

-sama: Conveys great respect; may also indicate that the social status of the speaker is lower than that of the addressee.

-kun: In a professional setting, this can be used to address a junior coworker, particularly one whom the speaker works closely with; conveys more familiarity or affection than *-san*. Used most often when referring to boys.

-chan: An affectionate honorific indicating familiarity used mostly in reference to girls; also used in reference to cute persons or animals of either gender.

-senpai: A suffix used to address upperclassmen or more experienced coworkers.

PAGE 57

In Japanese, the **id well**'s name comes from the fact that *ido*, the word for "well," happens to be a homonym for the Japanese pronunciation of *id* and can also be written with the kanji for *other* and *earth*, making the id well a literal "otherworld." In addition, the *ido* in **Sakaido**'s name is written with the more typical kanji for *well*.

PAGE 63

The **Wakumusubi** is named after a Shinto god of agriculture. *Musubi* means "creation," and he is best known for producing the kernels of what would become the five main grains of Japan from his navel, similar to how the device named after him manifests cognition particles. He is the twin brother of Mizuhanome.

PAGE 64

The **Shinsengumi** is a famous historical special police force of swordsmen that was active in the city of **Kyoto** from 1863 to 1869. Ryouma Sakamoto (1836–1867) was an influential figure who was murdered by a team of assassins at an inn in Kyoto; the identity of his killers is still a mystery, but the Shinsengumi were among the suspects.

PAGE 65

The **Kura**, meaning "storehouse," is the name of the covert police organization responsible for using the Mizuhanome System to investigate serial homicides. In particular, the word refers to a traditional, rural building used to house grain and other village valuables, in keeping with the agricultural naming theme.

PAGE 70

Paisen is modern, playful slang for "senpai"; using it suggests that the speaker is fairly young and on good terms with the person they are addressing (or just rather immature).

PAGE 72

Tokyo **Bayshore Road**, often abbreviated as Bayshore Road or just Bayshore, is a 70-kilometer stretch of road following Tokyo Bay through Chiba Prefecture, the Tokyo metropolitan area, and Kanagawa Prefecture.

PAGE 77

Fukui Prefecture is located on the middle-west coast of Honshu, Japan's main island; it is one of the least-populated prefectures and fairly rural. Hokuriku Expressway, the highway that appears in the id well, does in fact pass through Fukui.

Yakitori are chicken skewers grilled over a charcoal fire.

PAGE 80

Japan's **Metropolitan Expressway** (also known as Shuto Expressway) is a network of tollways that runs through the Tokyo region. It was first built in 1962. The Metro Expressway's **Bayshore Route** is a 70-kilometer stretch that bypasses Tokyo proper by running between the artificial islands along Tokyo Bay.

PAGE 84

Ooi Junction connects the Metro Expressway's Bayshore Route, Haneda Route 1, and Central Circular Route.

Saitama Prefecture and **Chiba Prefecture** are both part of the greater Tokyo area, north and east of Tokyo respectively.

PAGE 86

The **Central Circular Route** is a ring-shaped route of the Metro Expressway that runs through Tokyo's outer wards, lying about eight kilometers from the center of the city. The **Tokai Junction** connects Bayshore Route and Bayshore Junction.

PAGE 87

The **Mizuhanome**—the system used by the Kura organization to create id wells—is named after a Shinto water goddess, more specifically a deity of irrigation water and wells. She is the twin sister of Wakumusubi.

PAGE 90

Yamate Tunnel is an eighteen-kilometer tunnel on the Central Circular Route with one end near Ooi Junction. **Oohashi Junction** is a corkscrew-shaped junction connecting Yamate Tunnel to the Shibuya Route.

The **Tokyo-Nagoya Expressway** is an important, heavily traveled national expressway that links Tokyo and Nagoya. It's also known as the Tomei Expressway for short (*mei* is the alternate pronunciation of the character for *na* in Nagoya). From western Tokyo, the expressway runs west through Kanagawa Prefecture, Shizuoka Prefecture, and Aichi Prefecture, where it ends by the prefecture's capital, Nagoya, Japan's fourth-most-populated city.

PAGE 91

Yoga is a neighborhood in Tokyo's Setagaya Ward with a junction between the Tokyo-Nagoya Expressway and the Metropolitan Expressway.

Kanagawa Prefecture lies on the southern border of Tokyo.

PAGE 110

Odaiba is an artificial island in Tokyo Bay.

COMBATANTS WILL BE DISPATCHED!

AVAILABLE WHEREVER BOOKS ARE SOLD!

LIGHT NOVEL
VOLUMES 1-5

MANGA
VOLUMES 1-4

Always bring a gun to a sword fight!

With world domination nearly in their grasp, the Supreme Leaders of the Kisaragi Corporation—an underground criminal group turned evil megacorp—have decided to try their hands at interstellar conquest. A quick dice roll nominates their chief operative, Combat Agent Six, to be the one to explore an alien planet...and the first thing he does when he gets there is change the sacred incantation for a holy ritual to the most embarrassing thing he can think of. But evil deeds are business as usual for Kisaragi operatives, so if Six wants a promotion and a raise, he'll have to work much harder than that! For starters, he'll have to do something about the other group of villains on the planet, who are calling themselves the "Demon Lord's Army" or whatever. After all, this world doesn't need two evil organizations!

For more information
visit www.yenpress.com

ID:INVADED #BRAKE-BROKEN 1

Art: **Yuuki Kodama** Original Story: **Otaro Maijo,** The Detectives United

Translation: AMANDA HALEY Lettering: BIANCA PISTILLO

Yen Press
150 West 30th Street, 19th Floor
New York, NY 10001

Visit us at yenpress.com
facebook.com/yenpress
twitter.com/yenpress
yenpress.tumblr.com
instagram.com/yenpress

First Yen Press Edition: February 2021

Yen Press is an imprint of Yen Press, LLC.
The Yen Press name and logo are trademarks of Yen Press, LLC.

The publisher is not responsible for websites (or their content) that are not owned by the publisher.

Library of Congress Control Number: 2020950211

ISBNs: 978-1-9753-1773-7 (paperback)
978-1-9753-1774-4 (ebook)

10 9 8 7 6 5 4 3 2

WOR

Printed in the United States of America